# HOW TO POSSESS YOUR MARKETPLACE INHERITANCE

*Building Enduring Wealth using God's Methods and Avoiding the Danger of Temporary Success*

I0098971

**Charles Omole** LLB, LLM, PhD

ISBN: 978-1-907095-19-1

Published by:

**WINNING FAITH**
OUTREACH MINISTRIES

London . New York . Lagos

How to possess your marketplace inheritance

# INTRODUCTION

My objective in this book is to explain the imperative of our inheritance in the marketplace. It's important that when we speak about reclaiming the marketplace, we all start from the premise that it is doable. If it is not doable then the whole task becomes a lot more difficult. The righteous take over of the marketplace is not a pie in the sky or some unachievable dream. It is our inheritance as you will learn from this book.

I will be showing you through scripture that it is God's idea and that it is God's intention for us to reclaim the marketplace. The question is whether you will be a part of the end time move of God in this regard or not. You can be saved and still fail to participate if you do not rise to the challenges.

Many people have cut corners and achieved some form of temporary success, but that will not last or endure. This book will teach you how to avoid the danger of temporary success born out of partial obedience. The blessing of the Lord makes rich and adds no sorrow to it. So whatever God gives, it is perfect and complete. But that requires obedience to His instructions.

Living in a generation that is easily led by sight, this book will show you through the bible that you can challenge the old saying that "you cannot argue with result." You indeed can. It is not everything that appears to be good result that is God inspired. The enemy knows how to generate results as well; hence the need for greater discernment.

The kingdoms of this world becoming the kingdoms of our God is a task that will require believers to engage with the marketplace and dispossess the enemy of his spoils. The bible says that the mountain of God has become the garrison of the Philistines[1]

Well... God wants His mountain back. We are the people that God will use to achieve this. So the Lord declares in the Bible that we should ask of Him and He will give us the Nations as our inheritance. Whoever controls the marketplace, invariably control the nations.

---

[1] 1 Samuel 10

In this book, you will learn how to possess your inheritance, what the obstacles are and more importantly how to break the strongholds in the marketplace. You will also learn how to develop the right mentality for the task ahead.

This book is like a prequel to another book I recently published: *Operating and Thriving Behind Enemy Lines.* I will advise you read this book before the other one if at all possible. Doing so will give you the best context to fully understand the other book about the enemy lines.

To make the book easier to read, I have referenced most of the scriptural references via footnotes rather than in the body of the texts.

So sit back and enjoy the ride as we

journey into the Word of God to discover, who we are, whose we are, what we have, what we can do and where we are going.

Welcome to your inheritance in the Marketplace.

God bless you richly.

**Dr Charles Omole**

# TABLE OF CONTENTS

## CHAPTER ONE
### DIPLOMATIC IMMUNITY FOR THE KING AND HIS SUBJECTS - 13

## CHAPTER TWO
### THE ANOINTING FOR GREATER WORKS - 23

## CHAPTER THREE
### THE DANGER OF TEMPORARY SUCCESS - 37

## CHAPTER FOUR
### ESSENTIAL WISDOM FOR RECEIVING YOUR MARKETPLACE INHERITANCE - 53

## CHAPTER FIVE
### BREAKING MARKETPLACE STRONGHOLDS - 91

## CHAPTER SIX

## HOW TO PERMANENTLY KEEP MARKETPLACE STRONGHOLDS BROKEN - 123


## CHAPTER SEVEN

## DEVELOPING DOMINION MIND-SET AND MENTALITY IN THE MARKETPLACE - 149

# CHAPTER ONE

## DIPLOMATIC IMMUNITY FOR THE KING AND HIS SUBJECTS

God desires for you to receive an inheritance through your interaction with the earthly realm. The Bible states that thanks be to God the Father of Jesus Christ who has blessed us with all spiritual blessings, and kept them where? In the heavenly places in Christ Jesus.

The world economies are in recession, but we know that there is no recession in the kingdom of God. So how can believers live above the limitations imposed by this world's system? How can we live in Dominion as God originally instructed in Genesis 1:26-28? In the beginning, God created the heavens and the earth; but what for? Why did God create the earth?

Also, the bible tells us that our citizenship is in heaven. If this is true, then we must be on earth as diplomats and ambassadors of heaven.

This fact grants us Diplomatic Immunity from the limitations of earthly laws and practices, just like any diplomat enjoys immunity in his country of assignment. On earth, a diplomat is not subject to the laws of his/her host country. They are technically above local laws.

On earth, diplomatic immunity is a principle of international law by which certain foreign government officials are not subject to the jurisdiction of local courts and other authorities. The concept of immunity began with ancient tribes.

In order to exchange information, messengers were allowed to travel from tribe to tribe without fear of harm. They were protected even when they brought bad news.

Today, immunity protects the channels of diplomatic communication by exempting diplomats from local jurisdiction so that they can perform their duties with freedom, independence, and security. Diplomatic immunity is not meant to benefit individuals personally per se; it is meant to ensure that foreign officials can do their jobs.

We have been given assignments by God on earth; nothing on earth should be able to stop us from fulfilling our assignment. We are supposed to live above earthly limitations.

We are in the world, but not of the world. We are far from oppression. In a time of famine do you have to cut back and make do with less like everybody else? While the world may say yes, the Word says No! The Bible tells us that even in times of famine you can still enjoy the blessing and provision of God.

Jesus said, *"Many widows were in Israel in the days of Elijah, when the heaven was shut up three years and six months, and there was a great famine throughout all the land; but to none of them was Elijah sent except to Zarephath, in the region of Sidon, to a woman who was a widow[2]."*

Even though this woman did not have much, she still put God first. And God blessed her for that. He provided for her and her son during the entire famine, keeping them alive when humanly speaking it was impossible.

Your survival in a time of famine is not dependent on geography, on economic recovery, on a bailout package, on your ingenuity and skill, but on the faithful promises of God and your obedience to the principles of His Word. The Word of God says in Philippians 4:19, "*My God shall supply all your need according to His riches in glory by Christ Jesus.*"

Notice the supply available to you; it is

---

[2] Luke 4:25

according to God's resources, not according to the standards set by this world. There is no lack with God. Immunity from Babylon is therefore about how to live on earth with heaven's resources and assets.

## THE SPIRITUAL CONTROLS THE PHYSICAL

The standard of living of God's family in Heaven and earth should never be different. We are on earth as heaven's ambassadors. Everything that truly exists in the natural should be a physical manifestation of what already exists in the spirit if it is to last. The bible says, "Thy will be done on earth as it is in heaven".

In other words, what is happening on earth has already happened in Heaven. For instance, the bible talks about the

Ark of God in Heaven, the temple and tabernacle of God in Heaven, even earthquakes in Heaven; nothing happens here on earth that does not have its existence rooted in the spiritual.

Whatever you are experiencing, or whatever you have here on earth that is not a physical model of what exists in Heaven is not supposed to be your portion. So if they say you have cancer; is there cancer in Heaven? If the answer is no, then it means you are not supposed to have it.

The Bible says whatever can be seen is temporary and subject to change, but whatever cannot be seen is eternal. This means if the entire basis for the existence of something is earthly with no root in the spirit; then it is temporary and subject to change. But if it is a physical manifestation of a spiritual (unseen) reality; then it is eternal and yours for keeps.

It means the cancer does not have a spiritual root of existence. Its root is limited to the earth. Hence you can stand and declare that cancer should go because it does not exist where it matters.   It will have no choice but disappear. Also, that is why *"the blessing of the Lord makes rich and it adds no sorrow to it,"* because the root of the blessing is in Heaven.

The bible also talks about "laying treasures for yourself in Heaven" so that whatever happens on earth, depression, inflation or famine, does not affect you financially because your source is in Heaven and as long as the root source is not changing then your physical experience should not change. But whatever you have physically that is not a reproduction of what exists in Heaven then you can get rid of it. Hallelujah.

Living a life of dominion means living here on earth based on the experiences, the privileges and the resources in Heaven.

Understanding this will make you earth-proof in your experiences. Whatever does not exist in Heaven should not exist in you right now. It means before you get to Heaven (the Place), you are already experiencing it. Praise God.

There are certain battles you cannot fight in your own strength; it's not possible. You need to know where to go and you need to fine-tune the equipment that tunes up to that frequency so that when everyone will be panicking and you will just be calm and smiling. Understanding this prepares you to enforce your earthly inheritance in the marketplace.

# CHAPTER TWO

## THE ANOINTING FOR GREATER WORKS

*"The Spirit of the Lord God is upon me, because the Lord has anointed me to bring good news to the suffering and afflicted. He has sent me to comfort the broken-hearted, to announce liberty to captives, and to open the eyes of the blind. He has sent me to tell those who mourn that the time of God's favour to them has come, and the day of his wrath to their enemies. To all who mourn in Israel he will give: beauty for ashes; joy instead of mourning; praise instead of heaviness. For God has planted them*

*like strong and graceful oaks for his own glory.*

Then from verse 4, the Bible continues:
*And they shall rebuild the ancient ruins, repairing cities long ago destroyed, reviving them though they have lain there many generations. Foreigners shall be your servants; they shall feed your flocks and plow your fields and tend your vineyards. 6 You shall be called priests of the Lord, ministers of our God.*

*You shall be fed with the treasures of the nations and shall glory in their riches. Instead of shame and dishonour, you shall have a double portion of prosperity and everlasting joy. For I, the Lord, love justice; I hate robbery and wrong. I will faithfully reward my people for their suffering and make an everlasting covenant with them. Their descendants shall be known and honoured among the nations; all shall realize that they are a people God has blessed.*

*Let me tell you how happy God has made me! For he has clothed me with garments of salvation and draped about me the robe of righteousness. I am like a bridegroom in his wedding suit or a bride with her jewels. The Lord will show the nations of the world his justice; all will praise him. His righteousness shall be like a budding tree, or like a garden in early spring, full of young plants springing up everywhere."[3]*

In reading Isaiah 61 we find the true purpose of the anointing that is upon us as believers in this dispensation. Jesus Himself confirmed the purpose of the anointing that was in operation upon Him

---

[3] Isaiah 61 Living Bible (TLB)

by quoting Isaiah 61 in Luke 4.

*"Then Jesus returned to Galilee, full of the Holy Spirit's power. Soon he became well known throughout all that region for his sermons in the synagogues; everyone praised him. When he came to the village of Nazareth, his boyhood home, he went as usual to the synagogue on Saturday, and stood up to read the Scriptures. The book of Isaiah the prophet was handed to him, and he opened it to the place where it says:*
*"The Spirit of the Lord is upon me; he has appointed me to preach Good News to the poor; he has sent me to heal the broken-hearted and to announce that captives shall be released and the blind shall see, that the downtrodden shall be freed from their oppressors, and that God is ready to give blessings to all who come to him."*

*He closed the book and handed it back to the attendant and sat down, while everyone in the synagogue gazed at him intently. Then he added, "These Scriptures came true today!"[4]*

Let us read this scripture again in another translation:

*"Then Jesus went back full of and under the power of the [Holy] Spirit into Galilee, and the fame of Him spread through the whole region round about. And He Himself conducted [[a]a course of] teaching in their synagogues, being[b]recognized and honoured and praised by all. So He came to Nazareth, [[c]that Nazareth] where He had been brought up, and He entered the synagogue, as was His custom on the*

---

[4] Luke. 4:14-20 (NLT)

*Sabbath day. And He stood up to read. And there was handed to Him [the roll of] the book of the prophet Isaiah. He opened (unrolled) the book and found the place where it was written,*

*The Spirit of the Lord [is] upon Me, because He has anointed Me [the Anointed One, the Messiah] to preach the good news (the Gospel) to the poor; He has sent Me to announce release to the captives and recovery of sight to the blind, to send forth as delivered those who are oppressed [who are downtrodden, bruised, crushed, and broken down by calamity],*

*To proclaim the accepted and acceptable year of the Lord [the day [d]when salvation and the free favours of God profusely abound].*

*Then He rolled up the book and gave it back to the attendant and sat down; and the eyes of all in the synagogue were gazing [attentively] at Him."[5]*

While quoting the Prophet Isaiah in the synagogue, why did Jesus stop at Verse 3 of Chapter 61 when there were more verses in the chapter? It is very instructive how Jesus only read a small portion and not the whole chapter.

He ended with *"...announcing the favourable year of the Lord."*

Why did He not read further on? I believe it was because Jesus' earthly ministry would be limited to doing only those things that He was quoting: "*good news to the poor, freedom to the captives, opening of prison doors to prisoners healing to broken hearts.*"

---

[5] Luke 4:14-20 Amplified Bible (AMP)

That is why Jesus ended by saying that *"today this scripture is fulfilled in your hearing."* Good news to the poor, freedom to the captives, opening of prison doors to prisoners and healing to the broken hearted, all were fulfilled with Christ's coming. These embodied the ministry focus of Jesus.

However, just to make it clear there was still a lot more to be done by those receiving the Barton, just before His crucifixion, Jesus startled His followers by saying this: *"Most assuredly, I say to you, He that believes on me, the works that I do shall he do also; and **greater works than these shall he do**; because I go unto my Father."*[6]

So what is the greater works we are

---

[6] John 14:12

supposed to do? For a long time, many in the Church have been interpreting this wrongly. The bible states this:

*"How God anointed Jesus of Nazareth with the Holy Ghost and with power: who went about doing good, and HEALING ALL that were oppressed of the devil; for God was with him."*[7]

If Jesus healed ALL that were oppressed of the Devil; how many people will you need to heal in your meetings and crusades to do greater works?

If Christ healed ALL, there is no greater than ALL. So healing more people at our meetings is not greater works. Performing more miracles is not greater works, because nothing is bigger than

---

[7] Acts 10:38

ALL. So I ask again, what is the greater works that Jesus referred to that we will do? Let us allow scripture to interpret itself.

Jesus knew He could only do so much during His 3+ years of active ministry on earth and that we (you and I) would be the ones not only continuing doing what He did, but also going beyond and fulfilling the rest of the Isaiah prophesy from verse 4 onwards.

We are supposed to do the GREATER WORKS using the anointing that the Father has poured out on us to fulfil the rest of Isaiah's prophecy from verse 4:

*"And they shall rebuild the ancient ruins, repairing cities long ago destroyed, reviving them though they have lain there many generations. Foreigners shall be*

*your servants; they shall feed your flocks and plow your fields and tend your vineyards. You shall be called priests of the Lord, ministers of our God.* **You shall be fed with the treasures of the nations and shall glory in their riches.** *Instead of shame and dishonour, you shall have a double portion of prosperity and everlasting joy. For I, the Lord, love justice; I hate robbery and wrong. I will faithfully reward my people for their suffering and make an everlasting covenant with them."*

The same anointing that enables us to minister to people and see them restored, also gives us the ability and enablement to see our cities and nations rebuilt and restored.

I do not think we have fully embraced our calling yet when it comes to this Greater

Works commission. The greater works that Jesus was referring to is all that is contained from verse 4 to the end. This can be simply summarised as The SPIRITUAL RESTORATION & REBUILD OF CITIES AND THE MARKETPLACE.

This is the commission of the Marketplace Ministries. Occupying till He comes. Much of our ministries in today's Church is focused only on the individuals while the places and institutions within which those individuals live and labour remain broken and destroyed.

Peter later confirmed this when He spoke to the first believers saying that Jesus would remain in heaven until *"the restoration of all things, as the prophets have foretold."[8]*

---

[8] Acts 3:20-21

How to possess your marketplace inheritance

In the Amplified Bible, it is put this way: *"And that He may send [to you] the Christ (the Messiah), Who before was designated and appointed for you—even Jesus, [21] Whom heaven must receive [and retain] until the time for the complete restoration of all that God spoke by the mouth of all His holy prophets for ages past [from the most ancient time in the memory of man]."*

I believe part of the things that need to be restored is contained in the book of Isaiah Chapter 61 from verse 4 that we have earlier referenced.

Thus we can assume that Jesus will not return until we His followers fulfil the Isaiah 61 prophecy completely by not only ministering to individuals but to cities and nations, rebuilding ruins and restoring desolate places; by Reclaiming the Marketplace through the seven mountains and sectors of the Marketplace.[9]

The Anointing has been poured out on this generation for that purpose. Let us not waste it on limited application. Greater Works will you do. Let's get started with this commission.

The Marketplace which is at the heart of the nations has been redeemed, it is time to reclaim it. This further buttresses our claim to the marketplace as an inheritance.

---

[9] I have written a book that explains the seven sectors of the Marketplace in great details. It is titled: *"Breakthrough Strategies for Christians in the Marketplace."*

# CHAPTER THREE

## THE DANGER OF TEMPORARY SUCCESS

God stated in the Bible that we should ask of Him and He will make the nations our inheritance and the ends of the earth our possession.[10]

What God is interested in giving us is not just people (as in getting them saved), it is the nations (transforming nations). So if the nations are our inheritance then we must have a strategy how we get the nations. *'Your inheritance'* is mentioned

---

[10] Psalm 2:8

about 237 times in the Bible and it means *something to which one is entitled as an heir.*

But like all inheritance there are good and bad ways to acquire what is yours. We saw this in the story of the prodigal son. The inheritance was his, but he employed the wrong way to obtain it.

So there is always a danger of receiving our inheritance inappropriately. It is settled in scriptures that the nations are ours as an inheritance as we begin to pursue the "Greater Works" ordained for us by Christ.

While it is true that we are supposed to reclaim the marketplace, the methodologies we employ must be according to the pattern given by God to each of us. We cannot just go about this anyhow simply because it is our inheritance.

It is possible to receive what God has given you, (what God ordained for you) wrongly. And when you receive it wrongly you will get temporary success but ultimately it will lead to failure.

So we need to be aware of the danger of temporary success. The fact that you wish to do something God wants you to do does not mean a wrong approach cannot be taken to achieve it.

Let us look into the scripture for more understanding about this. The first example that comes to mind is the story of Moses. The Bible says and 'it' entered the heart of Moses and he forsook the palace and went to be with his brethren.[11]

What is that 'it' that entered the heart of Moses? I call it the force and call of destiny that is undeniable. The moment 'it' entered his heart, the Bible says he thought of being with his brethren.

Instantly Moses knew he was ordained to deliver the nation of Israel, but what was the first thing he did to actualise this purpose for which he had been called?

He went to kill an Egyptian thinking that that was the method of actualising the call on his life. Even though his perception of his call was right, his methodology was wrong. Hence he failed in that attempt.

---

[11] Acts 7:23

Similarly, there are lots of believers in the marketplace who are exactly like Moses. They know that God has ordained for them to reclaim the marketplace but they don't wait for a full revelation of His methodology to them. Sometimes, they may experience temporary success but you know it will not last. God is a God of precision.

Later in the wilderness when the people were complaining again that there was no water, Moses got angry with their murmurings.[12] God told him to speak to the rock to get water for the people, but due to his anger Moses struck the rock instead, thus disobeying God.

But if you read this story in the bible, a shocking thing happened. Water still

---

[12] Numbers 20

came out of the rock despite Moses disobedience to God's methodology. But he paid a huge price for it. That was when God declared that Moses would not enter the promised land.

A temporary success was achieved by using the wrong methodology; but there was ultimate failure to achieve a life's ambition of entering the promised land. This is the danger of temporary success. So, there is a wrong way to receive what was intended for you. This is a big lesson for all believers.

As we seek to possess our inheritance in the marketplace, accuracy is important. God's instructions to each of us will be unique to us. We must be accurate and use God's methodologies and peculiar standards revealed to us.

Receiving inappropriately and bad ethics, or erasing God-ordained boundaries and so on, may give some temporary success as you engage with the marketplace, but it will not last.

Engaging with the marketplace and reclaiming it is our inheritance. But we must do it the right way. And what is right way for you may not be right way for me. We must obtain our individual blueprint from God and not use another person's route to make our own journey.

The main challenge for Christians in these latter days are two fold. Firstly, many need to be aware of their inheritance in the marketplace (nations). Then secondly, there is need to engage with the marketplace based on God's SPECIFIC AND PECULIAR instructions to you. You must obtain your own blueprint from heaven. Your path is peculiar to you.

This is a real challenge for many believers. Many try to interpret God's instruction to others from the prism or perspective of their own journey. That will be wrong. Because God told me to do what He told you not to do does not make either of us wrong.

After all, God told Abraham to go to Egypt[13] when there was famine; but the same God told his son Isaac NOT to go to Egypt[14] when he faced his own famine. So who was right? They were both right. We must stop this idea that God has called everyone to do what He has instructed us to do. God is unique and has manifold (many sided) wisdom.

---

[13] Genesis 12
[14] Genesis 26

His wisdom is inexhaustible.

Lack of understanding of this principle has turned many believers into critics of their brethren out of ignorance. You cannot judge other people doing what God has instructed them to do simply by comparing it with what you have been asked to do. That is like putting God in a box and saying He has no other way to achieve His divine purpose. This is foolishness.

You must not assume God has only one way to achieve His purpose. Like someone once said, If you only have a hammer in your toolbox; you will see every problem as nail. Being blinkered by our own passion can wrongly make us critics of others obeying God in their own unique ways.

You must therefore avoid the danger of temporary success. Moses got water out of the rock by using the wrong methodology, but he paid the ultimate price for his lack of precision in obedience.

Another example of this danger is Gehazi,[15] the servant of the prophet. Through deception he prospered temporarily, but it did not last as leprosy came upon him for his manipulation.

If you don't do it rightly, you will lose your reward. 1 Corinthians chapter 3 verse 13, the Bible says, *"It will be revealed with fire and the fire will test the quality of each man's work if what he has built survives, he will receive his reward."* You need to engage correctly with the

---

[15] 2 Kings 5

marketplace to avoid the danger of temporary success.

Why is this important? Because your work will be tested by fire. And when your work is tested, if you have not built rightly it will be consumed; it's very important for us to understand the need to build according to the pattern revealed to us.

Temporary success could also be seen in the transient nature of some people in Christendom. They are in the limelight today and five years later, their names have disappeared from the news. They may have done the right things in the wrong way or with the wrong methodology; hence the problem of temporary success.

The crowd will applaud what they consider as success. But it is only the opinion of God that matters. If you were a casual observer of Moses, you would have assumed he pleased God as he seemed to have gotten the desired miracle...that is water out of a rock. You would have applauded him as an obedient servant of God, not knowing he had just disobeyed the Master.

Hence, on the matter of obedience that creates success, you must not be carried away by the praises of men who do not know the full story. Human acclamation does not mean you have obeyed God. Just as their criticism does not mean you have disobeyed God either.

If that is not God's method or you don't do it within the boundary He has laid, then you are going to have problems. God knows what He is doing and He is an expert at ensuring we are first prepared for what He has prepared for us.

The Bible explains the parable of the talent.[16] What many people don't know about that story is that the parable is not just about minas (or talents). In the parable, the master gave the different servants five, three and one minas. We see how the servant given one mina went to bury it and did not multiply it. In the end, the mina or the money that they were given by the master was just a test to prove the competence to rule over the real domain, the cities.

It was never about the minas. That was just a test. How do I know that? Let us see what reward the master gave when

---

[16] Luke Chapter 19

he came back? If you look at Luke chapter 19 from verse 17, the master says, *'well done, good servant, because you are faithful in the very little mina, have authority over ten cities'?* It was about cities all along.

It was all about taking over territories. We as Christians need to understand, that our inheritance of the nations is not about us just feeling good about ourselves. It is about taking over the marketplace. But God will use the little minas to prove your competence.

Think about it, from the little job you have at the moment, giving to God anything out of it is difficult for you and you want to take over cities. You must be kidding. For you to take over cities you must first come to a place where you believe and understand that God owns everything and you own nothing. You are merely a steward of what belongs to God.

It is important therefore for us to remember that the little experiences that we have in life are so that God can prove us and take us to the next level.

In the marketplace you must learn to engage correctly, whether it is in business, media, education, arts and entertainment or in government. The Bible isn't wrong when it states, "*unless the Lord builds the house, they labour in vain that build it; unless the Lord guards the city the watchman stays awake in vain.*"[17]

It is only the house that is built according

---

[17] Psalm 127: 1-3

to the pattern given by God that will last and endure. Therefore avoid the danger of temporary success that partial obedience could bring. Go for what will endure. Go for full and complete obedience.

# CHAPTER FOUR

## ESSENTIAL WISDOM FOR RECEIVING YOUR MARKETPLACE INHERITANCE

There are five essential wisdom principles or truths I want us to concentrate on in this Chapter that relates to our ability to receive the inheritance that God already destined for us. But before we examine these essential wisdom, there are certain foundational truths that must guide our understanding and operations in the Marketplace. These are the following:

## 5 KEY TRUTHS:

➤ **There is no Right way to do Wrong. A destructive means cannot bring about a constructive end. Wrong is wrong and right is right.**

➤ **Temporary adversity on that which is right does not make it wrong.** *[Joseph demonstrated that no-matter what the enemy throws at you, the truth in you will eventually give you prominence and victory]*

➤ **Temporary Blessing on that which is Wrong cannot make it right.** *[Abraham tried to legitimise Ishmael by circumcising him; but he was not the child of promise. He was eventually cast out with his mother]*

➤ **Two wrongs cannot make a right.** We have to stay with the truth and with righteousness. **You cannot dispose of wrong by eliminating the person wronged.** *[David tried that with Uriah* *after he had committed sin with Bathsheba his wife; but David's wrong became worse and not eliminated]*

➤ **The minority that is right will become the majority;** it is a matter of time.

With these truths guiding and guarding your heart, now let us examine the essential wisdom and operational truth that will help with receiving your inheritance in the marketplace.

1). **Every believer can receive an inheritance based on their work on earth.**
2). **You can lose your participation in Marketplace inheritance by receiving wrongly.**
3). **We can identify our inheritance by understanding our purpose.**
4). **We only receive our inheritance out of obedience.**
5). **Satan attacks us in the place of our**

inheritance.

So these are the five things I want to us to examine in this Chapter.

#1: The first truth is **EVERY BELIEVER CAN RECEIVE AN INHERITANCE BASED ON THEIR WORK ON EARTH.** Your reward is not just in heaven as some believe; but also here on earth you have an inheritance. God says we should ask of Him and He will give us the nations for an inheritance. That is, not in heaven but here on the earth. So you must understand that there is a reward and inheritance obtainable by you on the earth based on your operations here on earth. That is why God desires that we know His will for our lives.

One of my favourite scriptures in the Bible is Colossians chapter 1 verse 9.

The Bible says, *"for this reason, since the day we heard about you, we have not stopped praying for you and asking God to fill you with the knowledge of his will in all wisdom and spiritual understanding."*

The knowledge of His will, why is that important? Because the counterfeiting machine of the enemy has improved greatly in the last days. His will cannot just been known through physical eyes alone.

That's why the Bible says, *'if possible the very elect will be deceived.'*[18] Now, the 'very elect' will not be deceived if the differences are obvious. So we need discernment more than any other time in the history of the church for us to know that we can't just rely on seeing with the

---

[18] Mathew 24:24

57

natural eyes.

But some will say to you, '*see, I have the result to show for it'*; you cannot argue with result. I must be doing something right they will say. Well, that is not true because you can argue with result. The fact that a church is packed full does not mean God is there.

You can have church without God. Having result is not a sign God is in it, because there is the problem of temporary success as previously discussed.

But there is complete Satanic deception that can produce result temporarily. So do not get caught with basing all your judgment on seeing of the eyes. You need discernment of spirits to see behind the headlines.

## SEVEN SCRIPTURAL REASONS WHY YOU CAN ARGUE WITH RESULT

i.      **Nomatter the magnitude of the result, and the benefits it confers on the people, if the method is wrong it will become counter productive in the end.** *[God told Moses to strike the rock and water came out - Ex17:1-7 ; but then in Num.20:1-12  God said speak to the rock, but Moses struck it instead. Water still came out for the people (Result) but the* **wrong method** *used became the end of Moses' ministry]*

The people still received the temporary blessing of water supply but the method used was wrong; hence the harsh judgement of God. **The result Moses produced was not evidence of Godly obedience or divine method.**

ii.    You can argue with result because the Bible says so.

*"Beloved, do not believe every spirit, but test the spirits, whether they are of God; because many false prophets have gone out into the world. By this you know the Spirit of God: Every spirit that confesses that Jesus Christ has come in the flesh is of God, and every spirit that does not confess that Jesus Christ has come in the flesh is not of God. And this is the spirit of the Antichrist, which you have heard was coming, and is now already in the world.*

*You are of God, little children, and have overcome them, because He who is in you is greater than he who is in the world. They are of the world. Therefore, they speak as of the world, and the world hears them. We are of God. He who knows God hears us; he who is not of God does not hear us. By this we know the spirit of truth and the spirit of error.*[19]

Make a commitment to investigate the methods that produce the result. Does it line up with the word? Check the content and not just the package. The bible expects us to check.

iii. **You can argue with result, because the Devil is a counterfeiter.**
In Exodus 7, Pharaoh's Magicians also produced serpents from their rods just like Moses did. If you left the place at that juncture, you will leave with the impression that magicians of Egypt are as powerful as the God of Israel.

But we see that in the end; Moses' serpent swallowed the ones produced by

---

[19] 1 John 4:1-6 (NKJV)

the magicians of Egypt. **So if you did not wait till the end to see what happens, you could be deceived by the counterfeit of Satan.**

Then the Magicians of Egypt repeated several of the miracles of Moses until **Exodus 8:1-19** when they too produced frogs just like Moses. But Moses then prayed that the frogs should die from the house, but remained in the rivers; however, the magicians of Egypt could not do that.

That was the end of the magicians' enterprise. They could not replicate any of the future plagues.

iv.  **You can argue with result because the Devil is a Pretender.**
He will borrow the language of the Christians and speak as one of us. They

will even use the name of Jesus thereby deceiving many. This is why you need to investigate. An example is in the book of Acts.

"*Then Simon himself believed also: and when he was baptized, he continued with Philip, and wondered, beholding the miracles and signs which were done.*
*[14]Now when the apostles which were at Jerusalem heard that Samaria had received the word of God, they sent unto them Peter and John: [15]Who, when they were come down, prayed for them, that they might receive the Holy Ghost:*
*[16](For as yet he was fallen upon none of them: only they were baptized in the name of the Lord Jesus.) [17]Then laid they their hands on them, and they received the Holy Ghost.*
*[18]And when Simon saw that through laying on of the apostles' hands the Holy*

*Ghost was given, he offered them money,*

*<sup>19</sup>Saying, Give me also this power, that on whomsoever I lay hands, he may receive the Holy Ghost. <sup>20</sup>But Peter said unto him, Thy money perish with thee, because thou hast thought that the gift of God may be purchased with money.*

*<sup>21</sup>Thou hast neither part nor lot in this matter: for thy heart is not right in the sight of God. <sup>22</sup>Repent therefore of this thy wickedness, and pray God, if perhaps the thought of thine heart may be forgiven thee. <sup>23</sup>For I perceive that thou art in the gall of bitterness, and in the bond of iniquity. <sup>24</sup>Then answered Simon, and said, Pray ye to the LORD for me, that none of these things which ye have spoken come upon me.*

*<sup>25</sup>And they, when they had testified and preached the word of the Lord, returned to Jerusalem, and preached the gospel*

*in many villages of the Samaritans."*[20]

v.  **You can argue with result because you have only one life to live.**

You cannot come back when you are dead. If you are follow the wrong crowd you may not have a chance to change if you die in error. It may be too late for you if you do not act now.

vi.  **You can argue with result, because there is no Honest Devil in the Universe.**

The more you investigate error the weaker it becomes. There is no small evil. Once you recognise evil, then know that nothing good can ever come out of the devil no-matter how small it may seem. You need to be absolute with the truth.

---

[20] ACTS 8:10-25 (some verses have been omitted for brevity)

vii.    **You can argue with result, because nothing destroys faster than presumption.**

Do not assume based on title or size of ministry. The devil is still the devil regardless of his title. Samson presumed the power of God; but he realised too late that his strength had gone.

The children of Israel went to a battle without God's permission and took the Ark of covenant with them only to be defeated and the Ark taken captive. They fought a Presumptuous battle.

In fact, many of the satanic agents have the bigger and more visible ministries due to the attractiveness of the supernatural to the immature minds.

Many people simply equate all

supernatural happenings as coming from the Lord. They have forgotten that Satan was an anointed cherub . He too has spiritual powers.

*" For many shall come in my name, saying, I am Christ; and shall deceive many."[21]*

The Bible further explains:

*"Now as He sat on the Mount of Olives, the disciples came to Him privately, saying, "Tell us, when will these things be? And what will be the sign of Your coming, and of the end of the age?"*

*And Jesus answered and said to them: "Take heed that no one deceives you. For many will come in My name, saying, 'I am the Christ,' and will deceive many. And you will hear of wars and rumors of wars. See that you are not*

---

[21] Mark 13:6 (King James Version)

*troubled; for all these things must come to pass, but the end is not yet. For nation will rise against nation, and kingdom against kingdom. And there will be famines, pestilences, and earthquakes in various places. All these are the beginning of sorrows.*

*"Then they will deliver you up to tribulation and kill you, and you will be hated by all nations for My name's sake. And then many will be offended, will betray one another, and will hate one another. Then many false prophets will rise up and deceive many. And because lawlessness will abound, the love of many will grow cold. But he who endures to the end shall be saved.*

*"Then if anyone says to you, 'Look, here is the Christ!' or 'There!' do not believe it. For false christs and false prophets will rise and show great signs and wonders to deceive, if possible, even*

*the elect."[22]*

*"That we henceforth be no more children, tossed to and fro, and carried about with every wind of doctrine, by the sleight of men, and cunning craftiness, whereby they lie in wait to deceive."[23]*

As we have examined you can argue with result. Not all growth is healthy. Tumour is a growth, cancer is a growth. The fact that something grows, does not mean it is positive or that God is in it. You need to understand that there is a reward for you on the earth based on your work with God; but do not allow false growth to distract or deceive you into using ungodly methods.

You can't always use physical results to

---

[22] Matthew 24:3-24 (New King James Version)
[23] Ephesians 4:14 (King James Version)

determine God's ordination of an act. You have to be discerning; because something grows big doesn't mean God is in it, and because something is small doesn't mean God is not in it. We need to be careful that we have a knowledge of His will in our spirit and spiritual understanding.

Every believer can download and receive an inheritance based on their work on earth. Our inheritance comes from God, but we use our earthly work to bring it in. Hence, Kingdom wealth can never be acquired; it can only be entrusted.

Blessing comes before increase. God blesses you, then you increase because He has blessed you. In the same way, working on earth on its own will not make any difference in your life if you are not working from the platform of somebody that has already been blessed.

Standing on the understanding that you are already blessed, you now use your physical work on earth as an expression or a vehicle to manifest that blessing. Consequently, you are working on the platform of somebody who already has it spiritually. **God uses the earth and our interactions with the earth to bring our inheritance to us that is already ours spiritually speaking.**

Our inheritance comes from God. He is our employer and He is the one that rewards because He says a labourer is worthy of his hire. Therefore, the first thing is to understand that while we work, but we don't just labour and toil. Our work is a vehicle for us to bring in what is already ours spiritually.

God blesses you and then He increases you. It is very important—the Bible says, Abraham gave all he had to Isaac, that wasn't what prospered Isaac. The Bible says God later blessed Isaac. It was the blessing Isaac received that caused his prosperity, not the physical inheritance that came from his father.

So it is important for us to understand that working is important, but you have to work from the platform of somebody who is already blessed. That's the first wisdom principle.

#2: The second wisdom truth about receiving our marketplace inheritance is that **WE CAN LOSE OUR PARTICIPATION IN THE MARKETPLACE INHERITANCE BY RECEIVING WRONGLY**. In other words, any resource gathered wrongly is only temporary.

We can use our anointing in disobedience. In Numbers chapter 20, the Bible says Moses raised his hand and struck the rock twice with his staff; water gushed out and the community and their livestock were fed and they drank. But God told him, *'you will not see the promised land because you have disobeyed me.*[24]

He was in disobedience, yet there was visible result. This is the reason we examined the fact that you can argue with result in the previous chapter. The water that was the intention still came out because the gifts and the callings of God are without repentance. But we know he was in disobedience, because

---

[24] Numbers 20:12 (Paraphrased)

God said so. He said he would not enter the promised land as a result.

No matter how smart we are as human beings, our brain is like a tiny dot in terms of its capacity to understand the depths of our limitless God. We cannot simply rely on our reasoning to understand God.

Disobedience to God is always costly.

*"They soon forgot His works; They did not wait for His counsel, but lusted exceedingly in the wilderness, and tested God in the desert. And He gave them their request, but **sent leanness** into their soul."*[25]

In 2 Kings chapter 17, the Bible says,

---

[25] Psalms 106:13-15

*'the people fear the Lord, yet they serve their own gods'* This scripture did not make any sense to me for a long time. How can you fear God and still serve other gods? I mean it sounds like contradiction, doesn't it?

This exemplifies the state of many believers who are born again: they fear God but they still serve their own gods. They serve their own gods in many areas of their lives. God is not God of all areas of their lives. They fear God but they will still do certain things their own way.

They fear God, but they will still follow tradition. As a result their result is temporary. Again Joshua and the city of Ai[26] is another example of this truth. That's the first battle the children of

---

[26] Joshua 7

Israel lost. They lost it out of disobedience. So if you receive it wrongly all you will have is a temporary success.

**#3:** The **third** truth I want us to look at is that **UNDERSTANDING THE PURPOSE OF OUR WORK LIFE IS KEY TO RECEIVING OUR INHERITANCE.** Understanding our purpose is key to our inheritance in the marketplace.

In Matthew chapter 11 from verse 11 the Bible says, *'I tell you the truth, among those born of women, there has not risen anyone greater than John the Baptist, yet he who is least in the Kingdom of heaven is greater than he is'.*

I didn't understand this scripture for a long time because it didn't make sense. How can you say, among those born of women, there has not been one greater than John the Baptist. That means Jesus was saying John was greater than Moses, John was greater than Elijah, John was greater than David, can you see the challenge? Jesus said John was greater than all of them in the hall of fame of Faith.

Then the Holy Spirit opened my eyes to see that what Jesus was talking about is understanding life's purpose. Why? Because of everyone born of a woman, John the Baptist was the only human being that KNEW HIS PURPOSE even before he was born.

The Bible says, when Mary the mother of Jesus approached the mother of John when John was still in the womb, John recognized Jesus from the womb and the baby began to rejoice and leap for joy.

What Jesus was saying is that nobody born of a woman understood his purpose before he was born like John the Baptist. That's what makes him the greatest. Every other one I have mentioned, they are people who came into the full knowledge of their purpose after birth. Yes, they did brilliantly for God but John knew his purpose before he was born, that's what makes him the greatest of all the prophets.

Understanding your purpose puts you in a position where the grace of God can locate you for maximum exploitation of the marketplace. Your portion or inheritance in the marketplace is linked with your purpose in God. Hence John occupies a unique position in scriptures that cannot be beaten.

Jesus understood his purpose very well.

David understood his purpose too. The Bible says in 1 Chronicles chapter 14 *"and David knew that the Lord had established him as King over Israel and that his kingdom had been highly exalted for the sake of his people."*

In other words, he knew that everything God was doing in his life was not just for him as a person, it was for him as king and leader of his people. Early in his career, King David understood that God had blessed him for the sake of Israel, not just for his own benefit.

When we involve ourselves in activities contrary to our purpose we begin to sweat and toil in life, because when you move yourself away from your centre of expertise, you move towards your vulnerabilities. It's important that you understand that.

God has not sent you to everybody, he has sent you to a people or to a place, you need to understand what that purpose is and camp there.

You know, like one man of God says that McDonalds don't make hamburgers for everybody, they make hamburgers for people in a hurry. If you want corn on your hamburger, you won't get it at McDonalds, but that doesn't make McDonalds less successful because they are staying with what they do best.

We can potentially lose our marketplace inheritance because we are involved in activities God never planned for us.

When we involve ourselves in activities contrary to our purpose we produce dead works instead of the fruit of obedience rooted in our purpose. We get blown off course from achieving the intended destiny for our life. We potentially lose our inheritance because we are involved in activities God never orchestrated.

We need to understand our field; the field God has given to us. In 2 Corinthians chapter 10, the Bible states in verses 13 to 14 that *"We, however will not boast beyond proper limits, but we will confine our boasting to the field God has assigned to us."*

We all have a field God has assigned to us and believe me, in your field no one can compete with you; no one can match you. You are the best in your purpose.

We need to know what that field is and stay in our lane. If God shuts a door, stop banging on it. Trust me, you don't want to see what's behind that door; just allow God to lead you.

**#4:** The next truth is that **WE RECEIVE OUR INHERITANCE OUT OF OBEDIENCE.** We only receive our marketplace inheritance here on earth out of obedience. The promised land was received out of obedience, but prior to that, sweat and toil were common as disobedience dealt with the people. Provision always follows obedience; we need to understand that.

*"So I gave you a land on which you did not toil and cities you did not build; and you live in them and eat from vineyards and olive groves that you did not plant."*[27]

Jesus came to Peter at a time when you

---

[27] Joshua 24:12-13

shouldn't be able to catch any fish in the first place but because he obeyed we saw what happened.

*"Simon Peter climbed aboard and dragged the net ashore. It was full of large fish"*[28]

Provision will always follow obedience. There is a kingdom economy and we need to live according to that lifestyle.

#5: The final Wisdom or truth that affect your marketplace inheritance is the fact that **SATAN ATTACKS US IN THE PLACE OF OUR INHERITANCE.**

Satan is not omnipresent, he can only be present in one place at a time. Satan doesn't have the resources to attach to each believer one on one. He doesn't

---

[28] John 21:11-12

have the manpower. So what does he do? He chooses who he attacks based on his own priorities. The more valuable he considers you to be, the more he will prioritise his attack on you.

Hence, Satanic attack is confirmation you carry something of value. He will not waste time with you if you are going nowhere. So we need to understand therefore, that Satan attacks us in the place of our inheritance.

For instance, Jesus was tempted in three specific areas that relates to His purpose.

- The first was by his IDENTITY. — *"If you are the Son of God..."*
- The second was by his AUTHORITY— *by using His power inappropriately and at the wrong times*

- The third was by his STRATEGY – to accomplish His assigned mission. *"All this I will give you... if you will bow down and worship me"*

Attacks will come on the basis of the assignment God has given you, and you need to understand that Satan will only attack you at the place of your assignment. If you are in disobedience, he will leave you alone because he wants you to continue to be in disobedience.

But once you are in the place of assignment you will be attacked. You will be tested and you need to understand and believe in the principle that you can only win by righteousness.

If you do it wrongly, you appear to be successful—temporary success—and then everything will fizzle out. You need to win by righteousness. Whatever God sets you free from, He automatically gives you an anointing to set other people free from the same very thing. It becomes fruit of your inheritance.

God has set me free from fear of lack and poverty so you must be free from those too. Amen.

God will give you specific strategy that will become your key to your marketplace inheritance. The Bible is full of examples of this. God always provides specific instruction that will light your pathway to marketplace breakthrough. Here are some examples in scriptures to encourage you.

JACOB – received a dream to allow him to fund his family business and leave the employment of Laban.–Genesis31:11-13

DAVID – was given specific instructions to attack the Philistines only after he heard the marching in the balsam trees. 2 Sam.5:22

DAVID – received plans for the temple. 1 Chronicles28:12

PETER – was told by Jesus to cast his line on the other side of the boat; he caught lots of fish.

JOSEPH – received a dream and the interpretation which allowed him to become the ruler of Egypt under Pharaoh.

MOSES – was told the way to get water for the people was to speak to the rock. Exodus17:6

**NOAH** — God gave him specific dimensions of the ark to build.-Gen 6:14-17

**JOSHUA** — was told to walk around the wall at Jericho for seven times to gain victory

The Leading of the Holy Spirit is the greatest asset to a believer's destiny. To prosper in the Marketplace, you have to follow divine direction. Your marketplace inheritance will depend on your accurate obedience to the voice and leading of God.

*"I **will instruct you** and teach you in the way you should go; I will counsel you and watch over you."*[29]

---

[29] Ps 32:8

So every dream that God has given you so far is achievable. It is your inheritance; it is what God has ordained for you and it's time for you to take it.

God wants you to learn how to receive from Him in order to become a change agent in the MARKETPLACE.

God Bless You.

# CHAPTER FIVE

## BREAKING MARKETPLACE STRONGHOLDS

To fully inherit what is rightfully yours, you will need to fight some battles. As examined in the last chapter, Satan will show up to scupper your plans in the marketplace. So you need to know how to break the spiritual strongholds in the marketplace.

*"Nevertheless David **took the stronghold of Zion** (that is, the City of David). Now David said on that day, "Whoever climbs up by way of the water shaft and defeats the Jebusites (the lame and the blind,*

*who are hated by David's soul), he shall be chief and captain." Therefore they say, "The blind and the lame shall not come into the house. Then David **dwelt in the stronghold**, and called it the City of David. And David built all around from the Millo and inward. So David went on and became great, and the Lord God of hosts was with him."*[30]

Even after entering the Promised Land, Jerusalem could not be captured. Israel lived side by side with the Jebusites. The Jebusites remained in Charge (Joshua could not take it). Until David took the STRONGHOLD of the City in 2Samuel.

In the Marketplace, it is possible to appear to be making progress, but still have pockets of failure: pockets of

---

[30] 2 Samuel 5:7-10

containment that you are still dealing with.

The Jebusites *(the Blind and the Lame)* were the people terrorising Israel.[31]

**Until you overcome and take Strongholds, you cannot take hold of your Marketplace inheritance.**

*"Then David dwelt in the stronghold, and called it the City of David. And David built all around from the Millo and inward. So David went on and became great, and the Lord God of hosts was with him."*[32]

You cannot put your name or make a mark on your Marketplace inheritance until you overcome the Strongholds of failures, no-go areas and containment in

---

[31] 2Samuel 5:8
[32] 2Samuel 5:9

your life.

**A STRONGHOLD is a fortified place that Satan builds to exalt himself against the knowledge and plans of God.** Satan cleverly cloaks Strongholds under the guise of Culture

*"And David said **with longing**, "Oh, that someone would give me a drink of the water from the well of Bethlehem, which is by the gate!" So the three mighty **men broke through the camp** of the Philistines, drew water from the well of Bethlehem that was by the gate, and took it and brought it to David. Nevertheless he would not drink it, but poured it out to the Lord."[33]*

David had a longing....but there was a

---

[33] 2Samuel 23:15-16

**barrier** between David and the water of the well of Bethlehem. Three mighty men decided to Break Through the barriers to get the water for David.

**In the Marketplace; you MUST be prepared to Break through Strongholds and take over your Jerusalem. But Why?**

*"Lest Satan should get an advantage of us: for we are not ignorant of his devices."[34]*

To face an opponent and win a battle, you must understand how the enemy works. Failing to know your enemy may lead to a certain defeat. We are talking about a very sly invisible enemy here. We just cannot "hope" him away! Satan and his kingdom's mission is to destroy

---

[34] 2Cor 2:11

everything about God he can. His real mission is to target saints of God.

*Understanding Strongholds*
Strongholds spiritually can refer to two different things:

1) SPIRITUAL STRONGHOLD;
2) MENTAL STRONGHOLD

" *(For the weapons of our warfare are not carnal, but mighty through God to the* **pulling down of strong holds;)** *Casting down imaginations, and every high thing that exalteth itself against the knowledge of God, and bringing into captivity every thought to the obedience of Christ."*[35]

Since mental strongholds MUST be

---

[35] 2 Corinthians 10:4-5 (KJV)

pulled down. We must understand that spiritual warfare not only takes place in a large spiritual realm (principalities, powers etc.), but they also must be handled in the mind-set of an individual. Therefore, spiritual warfare can also be associated with warring with our own minds.

First we will deal with spiritual strongholds.

*"Finally, my brethren, be strong in the Lord and in the power of His might. Put on the whole armour of God, that you may be able to stand against the wiles of the devil. For we do not wrestle against flesh and blood, but against principalities, against powers, against the rulers of the darkness of this age, against spiritual hosts of wickedness in*

*the heavenly places."[36]*

*FIVE Hierarchy of Spiritual STRONGHOLDS (These are satanic offices)*

**#1: Devil/Satan himself.** [the MOST POWERFUL office]
The devil was originally a cherub, first in rank among the elect angels. In his own system, the devil represents himself as being God, but he is counterfeit.

Key to his success has always been and will continue to be the especially deadly combination of worship of himself (all false religion) coupled with the worship of live human beings (to culminate in the antichrist).

---

[36] Eph. 6:10-12

## #2: Principalities (Thrones or Dominion)

These are forces and dominions **dealing with nations** and governments; high-level satanic princes set over nations and regions of the earth; commanding generals over Satan's fallen army. These are the heads of Satan's world-wide network for administering his realm. They are the highest ranking of the devil's subordinates.

They sit enthroned throughout the nations of the world **posing as gods**. In the guise of deities, these high ranking members of Satan's inner-circle **receive worship from** men (instead of giving it to God). These are both National and Transnational forces.

## #3: Powers (Authorities)

These have authority and power of action in spheres open to them;

supernatural and natural government; high ranking powers of evil. These tend to be mainly National forces.

## #4: Rulers of Darkness of this World

These are governing the darkness and blindness of the world at large. They usually operate **within countries** and transnational cultures to influence **certain aspects** of life; they are governing spirits of darkness. These tend to be subnational Marketplace sectorial attacking forces.

They tend to exercise special powers of some kind. They would likely be the type of demon behind the exercise of pseudo-miracles and satanic demonstrations of power

## #5: Spiritual Wickedness

These are forces being directed in and

upon the church of Jesus Christ in wiles, fiery darts, onslaught and every conceivable deception about doctrine which they are capable of planning; the many types of evil spirits that commonly afflict people; the collective body of demon soldiers comprising Satan's gangs.

This is both the rank and file of fallen angels and the common name by which all of them are described.

Known by a <u>variety of names:</u>
- demons (Leviticus 17:7; Matthew 9:34),
- evil spirits (Luke 7:21; Acts 19:13),
- unclean spirits (Matthew 10:1; Mark.1:27), and
- devils (John.6:70),

The term "lordship" (small "l") is

employed for them in Colossians 1:16 and elsewhere (cf. Revelation 17:14; 19:16) because they exercise angelic, or "lordly" power, a basic function common to all angels vis-à-vis humanity until the resurrection changes the situation.

Jesus Christ, in addition to being King of the kings of the earth, is also **Lord of all angelic lords,** elect and fallen, from the highest to the lowest (Revelation 17:14; 19:16).

All these are offices of Satan and he delegates these offices to his DEMONS to carry out his wishes on the Earth. He can take on any of these roles Himself as they are all his manifestations. He can also choose to change their sphere of operation if he chooses. These authorities can be set over cultures, nations and regions of the earth.

*Key Characteristics of Demons*

The following are examples of the characteristics of demons in the Bible.

> *The demon EXERCISES HIS WILL, a **1st characteristic***

In Matthew 12:44, the demon who had gone out of a man says, *"I will return to my house from which I came."* The demon here exercises its will to make a decision, and then follows it up with the corresponding action.

> *The demon shows EMOTION, a **2nd characteristic***

In James 2:19 it reads *"You believe that there is one God. You do well. Even the demons believe - and tremble!"* Trembling is an outward mark of strong emotion.

Derek Prince wrote in one of his books

that at times he has seen a demonized person, who when confronted with the authority of Christ, began to tremble violently.

This may be an outward manifestation of fear by the demon inside.

> ➤ *The demon shows INTELLECT, a 3rd characteristic*

Demons have knowledge not derived from natural sources, rather from evil sources. The first time Jesus confronted a demonized man in the synagogue in Capernaum, the demon spoke out of the man and said in Mark 1:24, *"I know who You are - the Holy One of God!"*

It was more than a year before Jesus' own disciples began to realize what this demon had discerned immediately.

➢ *The demon shows SELF AWARENESS, a* **4th characteristic**

When Jesus asked the demonized man in the country of the Gadarenes in Mark 5:9, *"What is your name?"* a demon answered on behalf of itself and the other demons, *"My name is Legion; for we are many."* The demon was aware of both its own identity and that of the other demons occupying this man.

➢ *The demon shows their ability to SPEAK VOCALLY, a* **5th characteristic**

In the first three gospels and also in Acts, we see several examples of demons able to speak through the vocal organs of the people they were occupying.

The demons could and still do answer questions and carry on a conversation.

Normally we regard the ability to speak as a distinctive mark of personality.

Demons display a wide range of character traits. Some are vicious, violent, supernaturally strong.

Others are weak, cowering, even ridiculous--characteristics one would not expect to find in a demon, which is a fallen angel.

*How do Demons work?*
God can be everywhere at the same time. Satan cannot be everywhere at the same time. Since Satan was booted out of heaven, there has been a fight for dominion. Satan tries to accomplish his goal of dominion of your life through demons since he cannot be everywhere at the same time.

Satan dispenses or assigns his demons or demonic spirits to babies in the womb, people, families, churches, cities, governments, countries, hospitals, institutions, leaders, through music, through television, through drugs, through immoral sex, through perverted sex, through alcohol, and the whole of the Marketplace.

In very simple terms, God represents the light or the good and Satan represent the dark or the bad. Just as God and His Holy Spirit is active daily, so is Satan and his demons or demonic forces and principalities.

So far, we have looked at the hierarchy of Demonic manifestations. Let us now examine some biblical examples of satanic operations:

*Acts 16:16-24 — "Now it happened, as we went to prayer, that a certain slave <u>girl</u> possessed with a spirit of divination met us, who brought her <u>masters</u> much profit by fortune-telling. <sup>17</sup> This girl followed Paul and us, and cried out, saying, "These men are the servants of the Most High God, who proclaim to us the way of salvation." <sup>18</sup> And this she did for many days.*

*But Paul, greatly annoyed, turned and said to the spirit, "I command you in the name of Jesus Christ to come out of her." And he came out that very hour. <sup>19</sup> But <u>when her masters</u> saw that their hope of profit was gone, they seized Paul and Silas and dragged them into the marketplace to the authorities.*

*<sup>20</sup> And they brought them to the magistrates, and said, "These men,*

*being Jews, exceedingly trouble our city;* [21] *and they teach customs which are not lawful for us, being Romans, to receive or observe."* [22] *Then the multitude rose up together against them; and the magistrates tore off their clothes and commanded them to be beaten with rods.* [23] *And when they had laid many stripes on them, they threw them into prison, commanding the jailer to keep them securely.* [24] *Having received such a charge, he put them into the inner prison and fastened their feet in the stocks.*

FIVE SATANIC INSPIRED RESPONSES TO PAUL *(Be aware of how he fights back. He can do one or all of the following)*

1) Vs 19A – Dragged to the MARKETPLACE – **PUBLIC SHAME**
2) **2)** Vs 19B – Dragged to the

AUTHORITIES – **INSTITUTIONAL OPPOSITION**

3) Vs 20 – Put before MAGISTRATES – **FALSE ACCUSATION**

4) Vs 23 – Put in PRISON – **CONFINEMENT**

5) Vs 24 – Physical RESTRAINT – **PHYSICAL HARM OR PUNISHMENT**

FIVE SATANIC INSPIRED RESPONSES TO JOB *(Five dimensional attack of Satan)*

1) Vs 19A – Dragged to the MARKETPLACE – **PUBLIC SHAME** = *Job's Loss of Assets.*

2) Vs 19B – Dragged to the AUTHORITIES – **OPPOSITION TO OR FROM INSTITUTIONS** = *Job's Marriage and Family Destruction.*

3) Vs 20 – Put before MAGISTRATES – **FALSE**

**ACCUSATION** = _Job's Character Attacked._

4) Vs 23 – Put in_PRISON – **CONFINEMENT** = _Job's Isolation_

5) Vs 24 – Physical RESTRAINT – **PHYSICAL HARM OR PUNISHMENT** = _Job's Health Attacked_

Understand that the enemy will fight back

_"Are they ministers of Christ? —I speak as a fool—I am more: in labours more abundant, in stripes above measure, in prisons more frequently, in deaths often. [24] From the Jews five times I received forty stripes minus one. [25] Three times I was beaten with rods; once I was stoned; three times I was shipwrecked; a night and a day I have been in the deep; [26] in journeys often, in perils of waters, in perils of robbers, in perils of my own_ *countrymen, in perils of the Gentiles, in perils in the city, in perils in the wilderness, in perils in the sea, in perils among false brethren; [27] in weariness and toil, in sleeplessness often, in hunger and thirst, in fastings often, in cold and nakedness— [28] besides the other things, what comes upon me daily: my deep concern for all the churches."[37]*

**BINDING THE STRONGMAN:** Neutralizing the deceptive hold or enchantment that demonic powers have achieved over human subjects or Territories so that truth of God's word can be established and manifested.

So to make real progress in the Marketplace; you MUST BIND the Strongman.

---

[37] 2 Corinthians 11:23-28

*"Or how can one enter a strong man's house and plunder his goods, unless he **first binds the strong man**? And then he will plunder his house."*[38]

*" When a **strong man**, fully armed, guards his own palace, his goods are in peace.* [22] *But when a **stronger than he** comes upon him and overcomes him, he takes from him all his armour in which he trusted, and divides his spoils."*[39]

To Bind a STRONGMAN you need to come in the power of a STRONGER MAN

**What/Who is the Strongman?** All forms of Satanic manifestation as previously examined. Without Binding the Strongman, Satan will hinder you at some point in your journey.

---

[38] Matthew 12:29 (NKJV)
[39] Luke 11:21-22 (NKJV)

*"Therefore we wanted to come to you—even I, Paul, time and again—but Satan hindered us."*[40]

Thessalonica was big in Business and Commerce. Satan did not want Paul's anointing to come and mess up his plan and control of the city.

Understand that demons are territorial. Demons have Investments in Families, Regions, Sectors in the Marketplace and Territories. That is why they will do all they can to remain in their assigned territories.

*Mark 5:1-20 (NKJV)* - *Then they came to the other side of the sea, to the country of the Gadarenes. And when He had come out of the boat, immediately*

---

[40] 1 Thessalonians 2:18 (NKJV)

*there met Him out of the tombs a man with an unclean spirit, who had his dwelling among the tombs; and no one could bind him, not even with chains, because he had often been bound with shackles and chains. And the chains had been pulled apart by him, and the shackles broken in pieces; neither could anyone tame him. And always, night and day, he was in the mountains and in the tombs, crying out and cutting himself with stones.*

**When he saw Jesus from afar, he ran and worshiped Him.** [7] *And he cried out with a loud voice and said, "What have I to do with You, Jesus, Son of the Most High God? **I implore You by God that You do not torment me."** For He said to him, "Come out of the man, unclean spirit!" Then He asked him, "What is your name?" And he answered, saying, "My* *name is Legion; for we are many." Also he begged Him earnestly that He would not send them out of the country.*

*Now a large herd of swine was feeding there near the mountains. So all the demons begged Him, saying, "Send us to the swine, that we may enter them." And at once Jesus gave them permission. Then the unclean spirits went out and entered the swine (there were about two thousand); and the herd ran violently down the steep place into the sea, and drowned in the sea.*

*So those who fed the swine fled, and they told it in the city and in the country. And they went out to see what it was that had happened. Then they came to Jesus, and saw the one who had been demon-possessed and had the legion, sitting and clothed and in his right mind.*

*And they were afraid.*

*And those who saw it told them how it happened to him who had been demon-possessed, and about the swine. Then they began to plead with Him to depart from their region.*

*And when He got into the boat, <u>he who had been demon-possessed begged Him that he might be with Him.</u> However, Jesus did not permit him, but said to him, "<u>Go home to your friends, and tell them what great things the Lord has done for you</u>, and how He has had compassion on you." And he departed and <u>began to proclaim in Decapolis</u> all that Jesus had done for him; and all marvelled.*

*Key Lessons from this passage:*

1) In the Marketplace, you cannot

identify satanic manifestations / plans just through their actions. You need spiritual Discernment. Satan can do what looks right for a season.

This demon possessed man <u>was WORSHIPING Jesus</u>. Nothing wrong with that on its own. But you will need to look beyond the outside shell to see the  devil in sheep's clothing. You cannot wait for WRONGDOINGS to identify Satanic plots.

Something going wrong in the Marketplace is not always a sign of the Devil. Neither is something going right a sign of God's approval.

2) Regardless of what you say or don't say; SATAN Knows who you are in the Marketplace.

The demons in the Man knew who

Jesus was immediately Jesus arrived. You cannot hide your identity from Satan; even though you can to people. As you step into certain sectors in the Marketplace; the enemy knows who you are instantly.

3) **This man was destined to Rule TEN Regions (DECAPOLIS)**

But he was bound by six thousand Demons. Why so Many? Is that not an overkill? Great Destinies attracts Great Afflictions. The greater your purpose and destined successes, the more affliction you will attract.

4) **The demons begged to go into pigs. WHY?**

Because they had Invested in that Territory. They are not so much interested in the Man but in that territory. So they wanted to remain there anyhow. This is why demonic activities try to stay in territories they are massively invested in already. They are happy to move from father to son, mother to daughter, grandfather to son and so on; as long as they remain in that family. Satan is territorial and we must know this to equip ourselves accordingly.

5) **The delivered man pleaded to go with Jesus; but He refused. Why?**
Because the Man's destiny is connected to that province. He was destined to Rule TEN Regions. Once you win your spiritual battle, stay in your place of assignment and prosper. Stop running all over the place.

*How do I get demonic strongholds out of my sphere of influence?*

You can bind demons and temporarily stop their mission, which is to block you from receiving what God has for you. Why do I purposely use the word 'temporary' in this instance? After you BIND any demon, you should complete the process by **COMMANDING** each demon from your situation.

If you don't do this, then the binding process is temporary, which means each time you see the demon manifest, you'll need to rebind.

This can become laborious, so it just makes sense to complete the process by commanding the demon to leave. Commanding each demon active in your situation will not take place until you take care of the root reason(s) that gave each of the demons entrance into your circumstance or situation.

There are more supernatural activities and powerful divine movements taking place in that which is hidden than in that which is seen.

# CHAPTER SIX

## HOW TO PERMANENTLY KEEP MARKETPLACE STRONGHOLDS BROKEN!

*Breaking Spiritual Strongholds*
To win this battle and keep the enemy at bay, you need to understand certain principles from the Bible.

1. AUTHORITY BASED ON THE WORD. Every believer has the right to use the authority of Jesus' name to bind and take authority over Satan's activities.

*"No one can enter a strong man's house and plunder his goods, unless he first*

*binds the strong man, and then he will plunder his house"[41]*

**Firstly, identify your assigned Mountain in the Marketplace.** Issue a spoken COMMAND to the devil that he is bound and he **must leave** the stronghold! Don't just Bind but also COMMAND IT TO LEAVE. Exercising authority in the name of Jesus will expel the Devil's influence.

*"And these signs will follow those who believe: In My name they will cast out demons; they will speak with new tongues..."[42]*

**Study God's Word to discover how He will direct you to overcome the specific Stronghold**

---

[41] Mark 3:27
[42] Mark 16:17

**2. INTERCESSION.** Come together with other believers to pray and intercede against Marketplace strongholds until you get results.

There is intensified power in the gathering of more believers. Prayer with fasting intensifies faith, and faith will break strongholds.

*"Then the disciples came to Jesus privately and said, "Why could we not cast him out?... However, this kind does not go out except by prayer and fasting."*[43]

**3. DISPLACEMENT.** Establish the presence of God. Where Satan has been commanded to leave, fill it up with God's presence.

---

[43] Matthew 17:19,21

Where the presence of the Lord is, the Devil isn't! Satan doesn't want to hang around where people are lifting up Jesus in worship, in singing and prayer. The presence of the Lord displaces the Devil.

*"For what fellowship has righteousness with lawlessness? And what communion has light with darkness?"[44]*

**4. RESISTANCE.** Submit yourself and draw close to God. The Bible says this is how we resist Satan and he will flee.

The Devil runs from submitted, yielded Christians. He runs from your life, and will run away from where you go.

*"Therefore submit to God. Resist the devil and he will flee from you."[45]*

---

[44] 2 Corinthians 6:14
[45] James 4:7

**5. OCCUPATION.** Give no place or vacancy to the Devil to occupy.

With Satan departed, fill the void with God. Let righteousness be the standard rule and behaviour. Provide no pocket of rebellion, corruption or immorality in which Satan can find refuge to rebuild his influence or strength.

The scripture says to *"give no place to the devil."*[46]

**6. FORTIFICATION.** Clothe yourself with God's armour.

Take upon you daily, the full array of God's spiritual equipment that you may maintain battle-ready status. With the shield of faith, the sword of the Spirit

---

[46] Eph. 4:27

(God's Word) and the other links of armour (Eph. 6:13-17), you will be ready to resist any satanic assault and will be ready to engage the strongholds in others.

*"Put on the whole armour of God, that you may be able to stand against the wiles of the devil."[47]*

Satan will always seek opportunities to re-afflict. He is an opportunist. Don't give him room.

*"Now when the devil had ended every temptation, he departed from Him until an **opportune time.**"[48]*

*"And having spoiled principalities and powers, he made a shew of them openly,*

---

[47] Ephesians 6:11
[48] Luke 4 - 13

*triumphing over them in it."[49]*

We are more than conquerors in Jesus name.

*Breaking Mental Strongholds*
The mind of a "Christian Soldier" is the most important aspect of spiritual warfare. A person must be able to control their own minds first, before dealing with others.

*"Behold, I **give unto you power** to tread on serpents and scorpions, and over all the power of the enemy: and nothing shall by any means hurt you."[50]*

Spiritual Authority is NOT AUTOMATIC.
It is something you get as you develop in your knowledge of God and His word.

---

[49] Col 2:15
[50] Luke 10:19

But spiritual STATURE comes from God when you have overcome the devil and carnality in your own life. To gain spiritual authority, a person must conquer himself first.

DEFINITION: A stronghold in the mind is a spiritual fortress made of wrong thoughts, a fortified dwelling place where demonic forces can hide and operate in power against us.

The ideas and thoughts that make up the stronghold are based on lies that challenge the truth of what God has revealed about Himself.

Satan erects every stronghold he can in our minds to keep us from the true knowledge of God.

To the degree that he is successful, we

will not enjoy an intimate relationship with the Lord.

Satan's goal is to keep us in darkness by keeping us deceived about what God is like. His strategy is to distort our knowledge of God's personality so that what we believe is SINCERE but erroneous and inadequate.

Thus we are emotionally weakened and held in spiritual bondage.

## HOW DOES THE ENEMY CONSTRUCT A MENTAL STRONGHOLD IN OUR LIVES?

He starts with a foundation of lies, usually about the personality of God or about how God views us in Christ.

On this foundation, he builds brick by brick: vain philosophies, erroneous interpretations of Scripture, inaccurate ideas about the person of God, and distorted perceptions of how God sees us and feels about us when we sin.

Held together by the mortar of mistaken reasoning, the walls rise higher and higher. Soon lofty towers of stubborn pride and vain imaginations loom above the shadows.

Many Christians have vague, contradictory ideas about God's personality.

And our ideas usually come from our relationships with earthly authority figures. If we think of the authority figures who were the most influential in our early years, we will find that many of our ideas of God are connected to these people, particularly to our parents: fathers in particular.

*Putting on the Armour of God.*
The armour of God is used to fight against the demonic attacks on your life. They are listed here...

*"Put on the whole armour of God, that ye may be able to stand against the wiles of the devil. [12] For we wrestle not against flesh and blood, but against principalities, against powers, against the rulers of the darkness of this world, against spiritual wickedness in high places. [13] Wherefore take unto you the whole armour of God, that ye may be able to withstand in the evil day, and having done all, to stand. [14] Stand therefore, having your loins girt about with truth, and having on the breastplate of righteousness; [15] And your feet shod with the preparation of the gospel of peace; [16] Above all, taking the shield of faith, wherewith ye shall be able to quench all the fiery darts of the*

*wicked.* [17] *And take the helmet of salvation, and the sword of the Spirit, which is the word of God.*[51]

Here is a brief description of each and why is needed:

## 1) LOINS GIRDED ABOUT WITH TRUTH:

A soldier must know what and how to hold on to truth. We cannot truly defeat any wiles of the devil if we don't know the truth. Even the devil knows the truth, he just likes twisting it. We must know the truth to defeat him as well.

## 2) BREASTPLATE OF RIGHTEOUSNESS:

A soldier must live a righteous and overcoming life to be able to resist the devil. Notice that the breastplate protects the heart. Therefore, living right

---

[51] Eph 6:11-17

will help protect you from being defeated by devils.

## 3) FEET FITTED WITH PREPARATION OF THE GOSPEL OF PEACE:

A soldier needs to be able to fight spiritual warfare using the gospel. This can come in many ways such as witnessing and teaching. But, most importantly, always learning (preparation) more about the gospel.

## 4) SHIELD OF FAITH:

A soldier must know how to use his faith to shield himself from the fiery darts of the devil. The shield of faith is used to resist the devil. We must always keep it in front of us and not lay it down when we are discouraged.

Some things can only be overcome by facing it. Looking fear in the face and overcoming it takes faith!

## 5) HELMET OF SALVATION:

A soldier, of course, has to be born again. But in battle, one must also keep himself saved and standing. Salvation is a process; allowing God to change us (transform our minds) keeps us in a "saved" state. The helmet is to protect our thinking as the spirit of our mind is renewed.

## 6) SWORD OF THE SPIRIT:

A soldier must know how to use the sword of the spirit (the word of God). To fight spiritually and correctly, we must be able to rightly divide the word of truth and use it properly. It takes skill to use the word properly to defeat the enemy. You learn to use the word by studying and applying it to your life.

When a person maintains the armour of God in their life, they eventually will overcome self, the world and the devil. It does take some time. However, once a person gets used to the proper use of the armour, they will be able to get involved in spiritual warfare for others as well.

Fruits of the Spirit (Galatians 5:22-23) is critical for a believer. We must be Christ-like to help people overcome. Jesus had authority, but He used it with love.

Look at the life of Jesus; He embodied the Fruits of the Spirit… and so should we. In 2 Corinthians, Paul speaks about "strongholds." Another translation says, "strongholds in our minds." What are those strongholds?

*Classification of Mental Strongholds*

I will like to Group the Mental Strongholds into THREE MAIN THINGS:

### The first one is PRIDE.

The greatest stronghold of all in the unregenerate human mind is pride—**self-serving, self-preserving, self-exalting pride.** This pride exists based on Race, Nationality, Class, Denomination and so on.

### Out of pride proceeds PREJUDICE.

**Having your mind made up before you've heard the facts.** It's narrow. It's arrogant. And it's destructive.

### The third stronghold is PRECONCEPTION.

Thinking you know something that you don't, presuming to have a clear picture.

*"Because the carnal mind is enmity against God: for it is not subject to the law of God, neither indeed can be."[52]*

*OVERCOMING MENTAL STRONGHOLDS*

First, you **MUST find the law** in Operation in your life. On earth, everything works by Law.

*"Or do you not know, brethren (for I speak to those who know the law), that the law has dominion over a man as long as he lives? [2] For the woman who has a husband is bound by the law to her husband as long as he lives. But if the husband dies, she is released from the law of her husband. [3] So then if, while her husband lives, she marries another man, she will be called an adulteress; but*

---

[52] Romans 8:7 (KJV)

*if her husband dies, she is free from that law, so that she is no adulteress, though she has married another man. [4] Therefore, my brethren, you also have become dead to the law through the body of Christ, that you may be married to another—to Him who was raised from the dead, that we should bear fruit to God. [5] For when we were in the flesh, the sinful passions which were aroused by the law were at work in our members to bear fruit to death. [6] But now we have been delivered from the law, having died to what we were held by, so that we should serve in the newness of the Spirit and not in the oldness of the letter.*

*[13] Has then what is good become death to me? Certainly not! But **sin**, that it might appear sin, **was producing death in me through what is good,** so that sin through the commandment might become*

exceedingly sinful. <sup>14</sup> *For we know that the law is spiritual,* but I am carnal, sold under sin. <sup>15</sup> For what I am doing, I do not understand. *For what I will to do, that I do not practice;* but *what I hate, that I do.* <sup>16</sup> If, then, I do what I will not to do, I agree with the law that it is good.

<sup>17</sup> *But now, it is no longer I who do it, <u>but sin that dwells in me.</u>* <sup>18</sup> For I know that in me (that is, in my flesh) nothing good dwells; for to will is present with me, *but how to perform what is good I do not find.*

<sup>19</sup> *For the good that I will to do, I do not do; but the evil I will not to do, that I practice.* <sup>20</sup> Now if I do what I will not to do, *it is no longer I who do it,* but sin that dwells in me. <sup>21</sup> I *FIND THEN A LAW, <u>that evil is present with me</u>,* the one who wills to do good. <sup>22</sup> *For I delight in the law of*

*God according to the inward man. [23] But I see another law in my members, warring against the LAW OF MY MIND, and bringing me into captivity to the law of sin which is in my members. [24] O wretched man that I am! Who will deliver me from this body of death? [25] I thank God—through Jesus Christ our Lord! So then, with the mind I myself serve the law of God, but with the flesh the law of sin."[53]*

Death can be produced through what looks good. You can have GOOD without GOD (vs 13). Even though it is working against our MINDS the Law is SPIRITUAL in nature (Vs14). The Stronghold of the Mind, which operates through Canal Laws, can co-exist with an Inward Spirit that still serves God. (Vs15). This is an

---

[53] Romans 7: 1-25

important point.

You can be a believer who loves God and seek to do good inwardly and YET SIN DWELLS in your MIND. That is a Stronghold. (Vs17). Once the Stronghold exists in your mind; it will hinder your ability to PERFORM WHAT IS RIGHT. So, the mind will always command your capacity to act. (Vs19 – 20).

You must prayerfully through the Word, FIND THE LAW in Operation in your Life before you can deal with it. (Vs 21). You cannot overcome a Stronghold you are yet to identify.

The Mental Stronghold creates a BATTLE ZONE in your being. The natural/default Law of your Mind as a believer is Good. But the Stronghold wages war against what you know and believe about God. (Vs22-23). Strongholds of the Mind creates a DIVIDED You. (Vs 25).

However, there is a solution. Paul, Changed the Law operating in his mind TO **THE LAW OF SPIRIT OF LIFE.**

*"There is therefore now no condemnation to those who are in Christ Jesus,[a] who do not walk according to the flesh, but according to the Spirit.* [2] *For the law of the Spirit of life in Christ Jesus has made me free from the law of sin and death.* [3] *For what the law could not do in that it was weak through the flesh, God did by sending His own Son in the likeness of sinful flesh, on account of sin: He condemned sin in the flesh,* [4] *that the righteous requirement of the law might be fulfilled in us who do not walk according to the flesh but according to*

the Spirit. *⁵ For those who live according to the flesh* **set their minds on the things of the flesh,[how strongholds come in]** *but those who live according to the Spirit, the things of the Spirit. ⁶ For to be carnally minded is death, but to be spiritually minded is life and peace. ⁷ Because the carnal mind is enmity against God; for it is not subject to the law of God, nor indeed can be. ⁸ So then, those who are in the flesh cannot please God.*

*⁹ But you are not in the flesh but in the Spirit, if indeed the Spirit of God dwells in you. Now if anyone does not have the Spirit of Christ, he is not His. ¹⁰ And if Christ is in you, the body is dead because of sin, but the Spirit is life because of righteousness. ¹¹ But if the Spirit of Him who raised Jesus from the dead dwells in you, He who raised Christ* *from the dead will also **give life to your mortal bodies** through His Spirit who dwells in you.*[54]

## HOW DO WE DEFEAT THE STRONGHOLDS IN THE MIND?

**By Putting to death the Deeds of the Body.** Change what you Think About. Allow the WORD to Dwell in you richly. Bring every THOUGHT TO THE OBEDIENCE of Christ Immediately. Understand that there are NO INNOCENT NEGATIVE THOUGHTS. Endure Hardship like a good soldier. Putting to death the deeds of the Body requires DISCIPLINE, COMMITMENT, FOCUS and ENDURANCE.

Romans 8 goes further:
*"For if you live according to the flesh you*

---

[54] Romans 8

will die; but if *BY THE SPIRIT YOU PUT TO DEATH THE DEEDS OF THE BODY,* you will live. [14] For as many as are led by the Spirit of God, these are sons of God. [15] For you did not receive the spirit of bondage again to fear, but you received the Spirit of adoption by whom we cry out, "Abba, Father." [16] The Spirit Himself bears witness with our spirit that we are children of God, [17] and if children, then heirs—**heirs of God and joint heirs with Christ**, if indeed we suffer with Him, that we may also be glorified together."

# CHAPTER SEVEN

## DEVELOPING DOMINION MIND-SET AND MENTALITY IN THE MARKETPLACE

To walk in dominion, you must realise there will be opposition. But they are not powerful enough to stop you. Only your wrong mindset can stop you. You must see yourself the way God sees you.

*"For if you carefully keep all these commandments which I command you to do—to love the Lord your God, to walk in all His ways, and to hold fast to Him— then the Lord will drive out all these nations from before you, and you will*

*dispossess greater and mightier nations than yourselves. [24] Every place on which the sole of your foot treads shall be yours: from the wilderness and Lebanon, from the river, the River Euphrates, even to the Western Sea, shall be your territory. [25] No man shall be able to stand against you; the Lord your God will put the dread of you and the fear of you upon all the land where you tread, just as He has said to you."[55]*

Dominion is an INSIDE job. If it does not happen inside, it will not happen outside. Nicodemus asked Jesus... *"What must I DO to be saved "*. Jesus answered that *"except a man BE born again...."*

Nicodemus asked what to DO, but Jesus said what you do is not the main issue; it

---

[55] Deut. 11:22-25

is what you BECOME that matter. Once you Become, your DOING can then make sense and comes easy. You cannot walk in Dominion until you Become a person of Dominion on the Inside. You must see yourself as already having it before you can experience it.

DOMINION MENTALITY is a Mindset that is convinced of the reality of Kingdom worldview and irreversibly determined to exercise kingdom authority in all areas of life as commanded by God and His word.

So, what shapes the mindset of people.

WHAT ARE THE SEVEN MENTALITY / MINDSET SHAPERS?

1.    YOUR UPBRINGING
Your upbringing shapes your values and cultural perception.

"*Then the LORD turned to him and said, "Go in this might of yours, and you shall save Israel from the hand of the Midianites. Have I not sent you? So he said to Him, "O my Lord, how can I save Israel? Indeed my clan is the weakest in Manasseh, and I am the least in my father's house.*"[56]

Gideon's upbringing was fighting his ability to walk in dominion. But let's see more from Judges 6.

Vs 25 – "*Now it came to pass the same night that the Lord said to him, "Take your father's young bull, the second bull of seven years old, and tear down the altar of Baal that your father has, and cut down the wooden image that is beside it.*"

---

[56] Judges 6: 14-15

God had to make Gideon deal with his problem from its root by breaking the altar of his father. There are altars that can be erected to enforce weak and feeble existence that is contrary to dominion. Today, I break all such altars in your life in Jesus name.

## 2.    YOUR ENVIRONMENTS

This is the second Mentality shaper. God made Abram to change his environment before destiny could be fulfilled. So God said, Come out...

*"Now the Lord had said to Abram: "Get out of your country, From your family And from your father's house, To a land that I will show you. [2] I will make you a great nation; I will bless you And make your name great; And you shall be a blessing. [3] I will bless those who bless you, And I will curse him who curses you; And in you*

*all the families of the earth shall be blessed."[57]*

There are some environments that will not help you fulfil destiny. There are Poverty Mindsets. There are Mindsets of Limitation. If you live in environments polluted by these thoughts, you will be affected by them. Your environment can limit your potential

3.	YOUR LEVEL OF EXPOSURE
–*"Buy the truth, and do not sell it, Also wisdom and instruction and understanding."[58]*

Your level of exposure reveals to you what you will believe is possible. Whatever you don't desire you cannot acquire. Whatever you have not seen is

---

[57]Gen 12:1-3
[58] Proverbs 23:23

difficult to desire. Local minds can only relate to and desire local things. Stop being a local champion.

Travelling is a great form of exposure. Become exposed. Widen your horizon. Travelling enables you to see what God has done through others that will reinforce your dominion.

4.     YOUR ASSOCIATION
—"*He who walks with wise men will be wise, But the companion of fools will be destroyed.*"[59]

Your association will affect you in many ways:
- Your ENTHUSIASM can be affected by your association.
- Your TENACITY can be affected by

---

[59] Proverbs 13:20

your association.

- Your VALUES can be affected by your association.
- Your HABITS can be formed by your association
- Your PRIORITIES can be formed by your association.
- Your MOTIVATION can be formed by your association.

*"Do not be deceived: "Evil company corrupts good habits."*[60]

## 5.    YOUR VISION

*"Where there is no revelation, the people cast off restraint; But happy is he who keeps the law."*[61]

Your Vision will create boundaries around you. There are some things you will not

---

[60] 1Cor 15:33
[61] Prov. 29:18

do because of your vision. It will determine the discipline you will endure. It will determine the price you are willing to pay. You cannot become what you have not seen. You cannot have faith for what you have not seen. Dominion mindset requires Dominion Vison

6. THE WORD OF GOD (Spiritual Knowledge)

*"Be diligent to present yourself approved to God, a worker who does not need to be ashamed, rightly dividing the word of truth."[62]*

You cannot have dominion outside of the Word of God. The Word is your dominion tool.

*"Let the word of Christ dwell in you richly*

---

[62] 2Timothy 2:15

*in all wisdom, teaching and admonishing one another in psalms and hymns and spiritual songs, singing with grace in your hearts to the Lord."[63]*

Read the Word (Gathering Information). Study the Word (In-depth reading. Understanding the word more). Meditate on the word (Pondering on the word. This brings Revelation. Focused on a verse for a period). Memorise the word of God (Storing the word in your human spirit, that it comes to you readily).

7. ACQUIRED INFORMATION (General Knowledge Acquisition; Skill etc)

We are in the knowledge economy. Those who know will dominate those

---

[63] Colossians 3:16

that don't know. So you need to build your empire of the mind. Joseph did not administer Egypt through dreams. He was schooled in all the ways of Egypt. He produced a new blueprint in resource and human management for generations to come. Daniel was schooled in all the ways of the Chaldeans. That gave him the edge in the marketplace.

The Chaldeans were an intelligent and sometimes aggressive, warlike people. In 731 BC Ukinzer, a Chaldean, became king of Babylon; however, his reign was short-lived. A few years later Merodach-Baladan, also a Chaldean, became king over Babylon.[64] Then in 626 BC Nabopolassar, another Chaldean, began what would be an extended period of time during which Babylon was ruled by a

---

[64] https://gotquestions.org/Chaldeans.html

Chaldean king. During this time the word
Chaldea became synonymous with
Babylon, and we see many verses in
Scripture where the word Chaldean was
used to refer to Babylonians in general
(Isaiah 13:19; 47:1, 5; 48:14, 20).
Successors to Nabopolassar were
Nebuchadnezzar, Amel-Marduk,
Nabonidus and then Belshazzar, "king of
the Chaldeans" (Daniel 5:30).

At the height of the Babylonian Empire,
the Chaldeans were an influential and
highly educated group of people. So
there was no way Daniel could have
excelled amongst them unless he was
equally as well informed and educated
as they were. That was what He did.

At the time of Daniel, Babylon was the
intellectual centre of western Asia, and
the Chaldeans were renowned for their

study and knowledge of astrology and astronomy. They kept detailed astronomical records for over 360 years, which can help us understand how the wise men from the East would have been able to recognize and follow the star that would lead them to the King of the Jews (Matthew 2:2). Hence acquired Knowledge was key to Daniel's dominion in Babylon.

David explained how he was able to lead the people successfully by declaring:

*"And he ruleth them according to the integrity of his heart, And by the skilfulness of his hands leadeth them!"*[65]

As we come to the end of our journey

---

[65] Psalm 78:72 (Young's Literal Translation)

together in this book, I want you to reflect on all you have learnt. Understand that your mentality will determine your ultimate outcome. The more your mentality accepts the definition of who God says you are the more you will be able to possess your inheritance in the marketplace. God bless you as you shine more and more to His glory. See you at top of the mountains appointed for you.

## OTHER BOOKS BY DR CHARLES OMOLE

1. Church, It's time to Fly -- Learning to fly on Eagles Wing.

2. How to Avoid Getting Hurt in Church -- 13 Steps that will protect you and help create an atmosphere for breakthroughs.

3. Must I go to Church -- 8 Reasons why you must attend Church.

4. Freedom from Condemnation -- Breaking free from the burden & weight of sin.

5. I cannot serve a big God and remain small

6. How to start your own business

7. How to Make Godly Decisions

8. How to avoid financial collapse

9. Let Brotherly love continue: An insight into love and companionship.

10. Breaking out of the debt trap

11. Common Causes of Unanswered Prayer.

12. How to Argue with God and Win -- Biblical strategies on getting God's attention for all your circumstances all of the time

13. Avoiding Power Failure-- How to generate spiritual power for daily success and victorious living.

14. How long should I continue to pray when I don't see an answer?

15. SUCCESS KILLERS: Seven Habits of Highly Ineffective Christians.

16. The Financial Resource Handbook – UK Edition

17. Divine Strategies for uncommon

breakthroughs: Living in the Reality of the Supernatural:

18. Keys to Divine Success

19. Wrong Thoughts, Wrong Emotion and Wrong Living

20. Secrets of Biblical Wealth Transfer

21. Journey to Fulfilment

22. Prosperity Unleashed – A Definitive Guide to Biblical Economics

23. No More Debt – Volume 1

24. Understanding Dominion

25. Advancement

26. Getting the Story Straight

27. Overcoming when Overwhelmed

28. The Spiritual Fitness Plan

29. Spiritual and Practical Steps to Command Value

30. Breakthrough Strategies for

Christians in the Marketplace

31. The Seven Ms of Marriage

32. Supporting Good Governance in Law Enforcement in African Societies

33. Operating and Thriving Behind Enemy Lines

34. How to Possess your Marketplace Inheritance.

For more information about our ministry, world outreaches and a free catalogue of our materials, please write to:

Winning Faith Outreach Ministries
151 Mackenzie Road, London. N7 8NF,

www.charlesomole.com
Email: Info@CharlesOmole.com

# NOTES

# NOTES